Prayer
Without Borders

CELEBRATING GLOBAL WISDOM

EDITOR
Barbara Ballenger

PHOTOGRAPHER
David Snyder

CATHOLIC RELIEF SERVICES
Baltimore, Maryland

Prayer Without Borders, Celebrating Global Wisdom
©2005 Catholic Relief Services. All Rights Reserved.

ISBN 0-945356-16-1

Published by Catholic Relief Services
209 West Fayette Street • Baltimore, Maryland 21201-3443
410-625-2220 • www.crs.org

First Printing August 2004
Second Printing September 2005

Graphic Design and Layout
Karen Starr Adams

Printed and bound in the United States of America
US0577D

Contents

Foreword

Catholic Relief Services is pleased to present this collection of prayers, stories and reflections from the people we serve around the world.

As globalization shrinks the distances between people, the cultural and religious divide seems to grow wider. In the midst of all that divides the world, **Prayer Without Borders, Celebrating Global Wisdom**, stands as a testament that is at the core of our being: we are more alike than different. At the core of our being, we share the same concerns, dreams, and struggles.

We hope this book will inspire you, challenge you, and most of all touch your heart. Its contents show that the stirrings of our souls are truly universal. They transcend boundaries and cross borders. In the process, hopefully, they build bridges of solidarity. These prayers, poems and stories remind us that we are all members of the one, human family.

May you be blessed in the reading and praying of these heartfelt messages.

Joan F. Neal

Joan F. Neal
Vice President, U.S. Operations
Catholic Relief Services

How To Pray Without Borders

On my first Sunday morning in Africa, I sat on a hard bench at the back of a Catholic church in Tanzania. I was a soft American sponge soaking up the faith of a village. Soon I and the other members of our U.S. delegation were met with the loud unison of children reciting a litany, of the powerful harmonies of the choir, of drumbeats and ululation.

Because I am a life-long Catholic, the ritual was intimately familiar. Because the prayers and songs were in Swahili, I didn't understand a word. And so the space that I typically reserve for things I know by heart was filled instead with something more fundamental, more universal: the deep faith at the center of the prayer itself. For me, this was prayer without borders.

This book captures something of that experience on the church bench in Tanzania. The prayers, wisdom stories, poems and reflections included here flow from the spirit of people and places that Catholic Relief Services (CRS) serves throughout the world. More than 20 countries are represented. Much of the subject matter is universal: concern for family members, gratitude for blessings, requests for God's help. But there exists also an opportunity to reflect from unfamiliar, perhaps even uncomfortable, perspectives: from that of a Pakistani girl undervalued by her family, of a former Liberian refugee sorting through the shards of war, of a Vietnamese mother and child turned to stone from their long wait for a husband who never returns.

The book also includes prayers and reflections from U.S. citizens who have traveled with CRS and who are working to build solidarity between people in the United States and overseas. As the relief and development arm of the United States Catholic community, CRS offers programming in nearly 100 countries thanks in large measure to the financial support of Catholics in the United States. We also work with people of faith in this country to explore the reasons for poverty, injustice and conflict in the world, and to be a force for change.

The prayers and reflections that were selected for **Prayer Without Borders, Celebrating Global Wisdom** come from a spectrum of peoples and cultures. They also resonate with the faith and tradition of the Catholic Church in the United States, from which Catholic Relief Services receives its mission to serve the world's poor. The first four chapters reflect the four major seasons of the liturgical year: "Waiting In Hope" for Advent, "Welcoming The Holy Family" for Christmas, "Hungering For Justice" for Lent and "Celebrating New Life" for Easter.

The rest of the chapters feature themes that flow from the gospel, tradition and social teaching of the Catholic Church.

Within each chapter, the prayers and stories have been grouped into a series of brief sections. Each includes one or more texts as well as suggestions on how to pray and reflect on them. Additional information on CRS' work in the region can be found throughout.

The result is a prayer resource that we hope will be used in a variety of settings:

- In personal devotion, a different section can be selected each day or week to inspire reflection on global themes.

- In the classroom the diverse texts provide a unique opportunity to explore the spirituality and experiences of people in other countries, to learn more about the work of Catholic Relief Services and to discuss the call to solidarity.

- Individual prayers and reflections can be woven into prayer services or used to begin and end youth group meetings or church functions. Adult education or bible study groups can use the sections to foster discussion.

Most of the texts included in this book have been submitted by, sometimes even written by, CRS staff and the people they work with. Our sincere thanks go out to the many contributors and to all those who tracked down authors and secured translations and permissions.

–**Barbara Ballenger**

Waiting
In
Hope

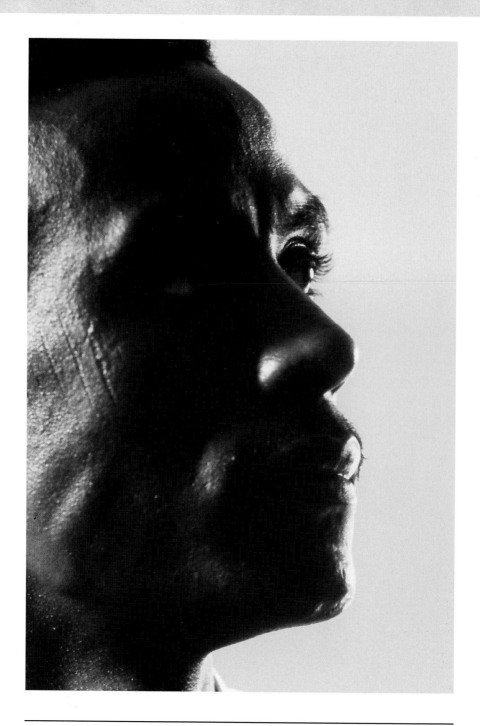

To have hope
Is to believe that history continues open
To the dream of God and to human creativity.

To have hope
Is to continue affirming
That it is possible to dream a different world,
Without hunger, without injustice,
Without discrimination.

To have hope
Is to be a courier of God
And courier of men and women of good will,
Tearing down walls, destroying borders,
Building bridges.

To have hope
Is to believe in the revolutionary potential of faith,
Is to leave the door open so that
The Spirit can enter and make all things anew.

To have hope
Is to believe that life wins over death.

To have hope
Is to begin again as many times as necessary.

To have hope
Is to believe that hope is not
The last thing that dies.

To have hope
Is to believe that hope cannot die,
That hope no longer dies.

To have hope
Is to live.

–Missionary Sisters of St. Charles Borromeo (Scalabrinians)
Honduras

REFLECTION: Hope is active. It does not sit idly by, but sustains us in the present while reaching expectantly toward the future. To have hope is to live, as the prayer asserts. In this Advent season, what do you most hope for? Who in your life is most in need of hope and how can you help them find it as the story of Emmanuel unfolds?

Grant Me Light

O God! Grant me Light in my heart, Light in my grave,
Light in front of me, Light behind me,
Light on my right, Light on my left,
Light above me, Light below me,
Light in my ears, Light in my eyes,
Light on my skin, Light in my hair,
Light within my flesh, Light in my blood, Light in my bones.

O God! Increase my Light everywhere.

O God! Grant me Light in my heart,
Light on my tongue, Light in my eyes, Light in my ears,
Light on my right, Light on my left,
Light above me, Light below me,
Light in front of me, Light behind me,
And Light within my self.

Increase my Light.

—**Muhammad**

God of our longing,
remember those who wait and hope for peace.
Hear our prayer and our lament
for our brothers and sisters in Israel and Palestine.
With them we share a common story, set in a common homeland.

Make common also a will to forgive, to reconcile,
to make a just peace for the sake of the ancestors,
for the sake of the children.
Open ears, eyes and hearts
and make a way toward justice in our war-torn world.

God all merciful, you dwell in human hearts
and the Holy Land is wherever you make your home.
Heal these broken places where prophets preached,
where Moses and Jesus and Muhammad kept faith with you.
Be a sure support for those who work toward reconciliation
and make us all, however far away, steadfast in their cause.

−Catholic Relief Services
USA

It is our job to remove the peasants from the cross (Liberation Theology) − change society so they aren't poor − have a away team a job etc

REFLECTION: In the weeks leading up to Christmas, leave a special place in your prayer for all who are caught up in violence in the Holy Land, as well as for those who are striving to foster peace and reconciliation among the Jews, Muslims and Christians who live there.

About Catholic Relief Services: CRS began implementing projects in Palestine in the late 1940s, and opened an office in Jerusalem in 1961. Since that time CRS has provided programming in Jerusalem, the West Bank and Gaza Strip, which are home to some of the area's most vulnerable people, many of whom have been refugees for more than 50 years. In 2004, CRS worked with the 3.6 million Palestinians living in the region, creating jobs while improving basic community services, providing emergency assistance, and establishing youth centers to help children overcome the isolation and psychological trauma of the ongoing conflict there.

9

The Lion's Whisker

Long ago in Ethiopia, a woman married a widower who had a son. Her joy was great when she went to live in the home of her new husband, for she longed for a child. But the child refused her affections, saying, "You are not my mother." He refused her cooking, tore her mending, and turned away from her kindness.

After some time, the sorrowing woman decided to seek the help of a wise hermit who lived on the mountain. "Make me a potion," she begged, "so my stepson will love me as I love him."

"I can make such a potion," he said, "but the ingredients are very difficult to obtain. You must bring me a whisker of a living lion."

The woman went away in great distress but determined not to give up. That night, while her family slept, she crept out of the village to the edge of the desert carrying a bowl of meat. She knew that a great lion lived near some rocks quite a distance away. She walked under the night sky as close to the lion as she dared. Hearing him roar, she dropped the bowl and ran back home. Again the next night, she sneaked from the house with a bowl of meat. She walked farther into the desert until she could see the form of the lion on the distant rocks. She set down her bowl and ran home.

Every night she drew closer to the lion before setting down her bowl and fleeing for home. Every night the lion ate her food. Finally one night, after many weeks, she placed down her bowl and stepped back but did not run. She watched the huge cat come slowly forward and eat from the bowl. The following night, she placed down the bowl and did not move away. The lion came slowly forward and began to eat from the bowl. She reached out and stroked his fur. He made happy sounds in his throat. "Thank you, dear friend," she said, and carefully snipped a whisker from his chin. She moved slowly away and then ran all the way to the wise hermit's hut.

"I've bought you the whisker of a living lion," she called, running into his hut. The hermit was sitting before his fire. He took the whisker and examined it closely. "You have indeed," he said, and dropped the whisker into the fire.

"What have you done?" she cried. "That was the whisker for the love potion. You don't know how hard it was to obtain. It has taken me months to win the trust of the lion."

"Can the love and trust of a child be harder to obtain than that of a wild beast?" he asked her. "Go home and think on what you have done."

The woman returned home and slowly, with love and patience, won the trust and love of her stepson.

–Ethiopia

REFLECTION: Solidarity with the poor is a long-term relationship. Understanding the intricacies of the root causes of poverty, witnessing first hand the struggle and stories of people in poverty, and working to change complex systems of injustice require as much determination and courage as the woman's quest to pluck the whisker from the chin of a lion. Her motivation is love. What do you need to sustain such a relationship with the poor? Share your need with God.

Pilgrim From Birth

We walk, Lord, guided as pilgrims,
with confidence that your presence gives us life,
and is stronger than the weariness of the road.

When we walk, Lord,
we know that you keep your promises,
that a seedling of hope
has sprung up in the midst of a dry people.

We walk, Lord, with our hands empty,
seeking to be filled with your presence.
We go full of poverty to be enriched.

–Mexico

Light shines on the way, God my companion.
Come, guide the footsteps of the people for new destinations!
Defend us from danger, protect us!

Light shines each day on the journey, O God.
Come, lift up those who have fallen, to heal their wounds!
Bring justice for the forgotten multitudes!
Everything changes with your love. We too are divine!

Light shines in history, O God of memory.
Come, make new our covenant and our hope!
The gospel of your Son gives new light to the people.
May your grace forgive us and bless us.

–Missionary Sisters of St. Charles Borromeo (Scalabrinians)
Honduras

O Christ, pilgrim before birth,
you made your life a march of meetings with others.
Not knowing where to rest your head,
you wanted every person, all of us pilgrims,
to have hope.

We bring to you the needs of all migrants:
Give them a place that will nourish them
and will make them strong of heart, firm in their identity.
Help them to live in justice,
in solidarity, and in peace.
In your love see that they are welcomed.
All are made in your image,
all are bound toward community
with sisters and brothers in the faith.

May they not walk more than necessary,
and when they halt
may their walking not be in vain.
May we migrants all be blessed as the world is blessed.

Amen.

—Missionary Sisters of St. Charles Borromeo (Scalabrinians)
Honduras

REFLECTION: When people live in poverty, they walk—sometimes considerable distances. Consider the long march of refugees fleeing conflict, the daily travel that women and children make to distant water sources, and the way that the urban poor trek through cities and wait for crowded public transportation. In your prayer, ask God how you can share the walk of the poor. As an act of solidarity, spend a day walking and using public transportation to reach the places you need to go.

About Catholic Relief Services: Along Mexico's border, more than 2,500 people have died attempting to enter the United States undetected since 1994. CRS-Mexico helps Mexicans achieve economic stability so that they do not need to leave their country to find work. That includes helping Mexican farmers improve their working conditions, inviting dialogue between small farmers in the U.S. and Mexico to understand their shared concerns and supporting the local church as it reaches out to vulnerable migrants along the border.

WELCOMING

THE HOLY FAMILY

Of Innocents And Exile

Most holy Virgin Mary,
on the roads of the world
you accompany those who immigrate
in search of work and sustenance.

You also knew exile.
Look at us with compassion and bless those who receive us.
Protect those that need disperses and love gathers
in the midst of their own sweat
and the hard fatigues of life.

You, help of Christians,
console the afflicted.
Be the loving mother of those who by necessity
live far from their land.

Be the mother of those who struggle anxiously for their needs
without finding someone who understands their sufferings.
Revive their strength and lift their battered spirits
with your voice of encouragement.

Comfort with mercy,
aid with your mother's care,
defend by your intercession!

O Mary, make us, the migrants and our families,
walk by faith, by hope and charity.
Make us walk in holy fear of God
while trusting in God's will,
ever faithful to Jesus Christ and to this church.
Help us, Mary, to obtain the fruits of Christian justice
and so merit peace in this life and eternal happiness.

—Pope Pius XII

The road to Egypt was long and the journey wearisome. Joseph walked in front to show the way, and Mary walked behind with Salome, who had followed them to Egypt.

Sometimes Mary carried the child on her back, sometimes on her shoulders, and sometimes in her arms, and sometimes Salome carried him in turn.

Mary would set him down on the ground to walk by himself, and he would walk a little way at a time, holding the hem of her skirt. Then he would lift up his arms, as children do who ask their mothers to carry them, and Mary would pick him up and kiss and carry him again.

Joseph's heart grew tried because of the length of the road. "I am too old," he said. "I cannot go on."

But Mary put the child into his arms, and Joseph lifted him onto his shoulder, and he forgot that he was tired. He kissed the child from his head to his feet and went on again, with new strength.

—Ethiopia

REFLECTION: Stories of refugees and exiles can be found throughout Hebrew and Christian scriptures. Consider how stories of the Holy Family's own flight from violence must resonate with refugees throughout the world. Pray for those who are fleeing conflict, oppression and poverty. In what ways can you welcome such people who come to live in your community?

About Catholic Relief Services: In Ethiopia, where drought often leads to famine, CRS works with farming and herding communities to develop new agricultural techniques that resist the inconsistencies of the weather. It can be long, labor-intensive work as community members build by hand miles of low, stone terrace walls that prevent erosion and catch soil on the rocky hillsides. The resulting water systems and planting approaches are owned, run and managed by the communities.

My Burden Is Light

O Jesus, I pray for those who wander far from their homeland
and live the lives of migrants.
They are our brothers and sisters,
refugees who flee from violence,
families on the road because of poverty.
None of them know where to arrive.
All of them need your help!

You know them
for you yourself experienced the hard days of exile
together with Mary and Joseph.

Our migrant sisters and brothers need your light
to uncover the empty promises that frequently attract them.
They need your church to remind them of their obligations,
often forgotten in their daily sufferings.
They need your help
to ennoble and to confirm them as Christians in their work.

Heart of Jesus, bless the migrants,
and fill their lives with the love of God
from whom all good things come.

Defend them from danger.
Make strong their faith
to seek happiness not only in this world, but also for eternal life.
As pilgrims, as the church itself,
may they reach the heavenly city and be with you forever.

Amen.

—**Missionary Sisters of St. Charles Borromeo (Scalabrinians)**
Mexico

May no family begin abruptly.
May no family end for lack of love.
May the couple be one in body and mind
and may no one in the world tear a home to pieces.

May no family sleep under a bridge,
and may no one interfere in the life and in the peace of the two.
Nor should anyone make a family live without any horizon,
but may the family live without fear of what comes later.

May the family know why and where it goes.
May the husband carry the grace of being a father.
May the wife be heaven and tenderness and strength and warmth.
May the children know the strength that love brings.

Bless, O Lord, the families! Amen.
Bless, O Lord, my family!

May husband and wife have the strength to love without measure.
May they not go to bed without seeking pardon.
May infants know the gift of love
and the family celebrate the miracle of kisses and of bread.

May husband and wife on their knees contemplate their children.
May they find in those children the strength to continue.
May the brightest star in the heavens
be the star of hope for peace and the certainty of loving.

–Diocese of Juigalpa
Nicaragua

REFLECTION: This prayer from Nicaragua rings with a startling vision of all that makes for a holy family. Read the prayer again, then sit quietly for a few moments and let an image of a family form in your mind. Study the members' faces, notice their surroundings. Reverently, keep company with this holy family for a while. Close your time together with a simple "Amen."

O Lord Jesus, you knew the bitterness of exile.
With Mary and Joseph you had to seek refuge in a foreign land.
You understand that my soul is torn by bitterness
for I must leave those I love.

I am to cross the border without documents.
This search for a better future for my family makes me cross.

I feel a citizen of the world
and I am of the church with no borders.
I ask you, Lord, to allow me to reach my destination
without hard times, without obstacles.
You know well that I want the tranquility
and the peace of all.

Guide my steps
and give me the strength necessary to confront
the challenges that await me.
Your will and not mine be done.

—Missionary Sisters of St. Charles Borromeo (Scalabrinians)
Mexico

REFLECTION: "I am of the church with no borders," observes the narrator of the second prayer. The members are those that "need disperses and love gathers." What does it mean to view church in this way? Do you count yourself as a member? Who in your own community are "of the church with no borders"? Prayerfully reflect on the ways that God may be calling you to be of this church, as well.

About Catholic Relief Services: More than 45 million people are displaced throughout the world today, according to United Nations statistics. Of these, 25 million are internally displaced within their countries and more than 20 million are refugees who have fled to other countries. From its earliest days responding to Europe's World War II refugees, CRS has worked to help displaced persons from Kosovo to Sudan to Afghanistan return, rebuild and re-establish peace and stability in their communities.

Borders Made By Human Hands

There was a couple. The husband went to the front. The wife held the child to see the husband off. Year after year, the husband did not come home. He had died while fighting in the front.

The wife was so grieved that every day she held the child and climbed to the top the mountain to look toward the front, desperately hoping to see her husband coming home. She and the child stood on the top of the mountain and did not want to come home. The wife and the child stood, immovable, on the mountain for so long that they were petrified. They became what people call the "waiting for husband stone."

—Vietnam

Mary, mother of the poor:
    Help us bear peace to the world.
Laboring mother at the bolted door:
    Help us bear peace to the world.
Mother who fled to safety with her child:
    Help us bear peace to the world.
Mother who saw the death of holy innocents:
    Help us bear peace to the world.

Bearer of the Christ:
    Help us bear peace to the world.
Bearer of immense responsibility:
    Help us bear peace to the world.
Bearer of the light of possibility:
    Help us bear peace to the world.
Bearer of the good news:
    Help us bear peace to the world.

Woman who said yes to the divine:
    Help us bear peace to the world.
Woman who pondered miracles in her heart:
    Help us bear peace to the world.
Woman arrayed with confidence:
    Help us bear peace to the world.
Woman clothed in undying faith:
    Help us bear peace to the world.

–Catholic Relief Services
USA

REFLECTION: From significant stone outcroppings to the carved statues of cathedrals, monuments sustain memory. Picture the "waiting for husband stone" on its mountain in Vietnam. In praying the Marian litany, remember those who wait for loved ones who have disappeared; who wait for food, clean water, and medicine that has yet to be delivered; who wait for healing and reconciliation where conflict still resides; who wait for their dignity to be recognized. How will you bear peace to this waiting world?

About Catholic Relief Services: Vietnam has a population of more than 77 million. The majority lives in rural areas and is dependent on agriculture for a living. Decades of conflict ending in 1990 have left infrastructure underdeveloped or in disrepair. Since 1994, CRS has been supporting the efforts of local communities to improve education, strengthen agriculture and land use, and help poor rural families improve their livelihoods.

Blessed Are

Blessed are those who are on the move,
transforming exodus and flight in energy for a new search.
From the victims will come the protagonists of history.

Blessed are those who, forced to wander without direction,
with wisdom learn and teach the lessons of the road.
They will be the architects of a new time.

Blessed are those who suffer pain, nostalgia and loneliness,
yet know how to make of every arrival a new beginning.
They shall act with faith, hope and life.

Blessed are those who open borders
and mix the anthems, flags, races and creeds.
Without discrimination, they make the world everyone's home.

Blessed the wayfarers of all roads
in the tears, sweat and the work of their hands.
They prepare a tomorrow of justice and right.

Blessed are those who open the door to pilgrims,
making solidarity the passport to our common homeland.
They are constructing a new citizenship.

Blessed are those who foment encounters and re-encounters,
sowing peace.
They will harvest flowers and stars in the new heaven and the new earth.

Blessed are the excluded, without opportunities and without voice.
They will be the first guests in the great banquet,
where bread will not be lacking on anyone's table.

–Fr. José Alfredo Goncalves
Brazil

From heaven one beautiful morning
the Guadalupana came down to Tepeyac.

She joined her hands in prayer
and her face and her features were those of the native peoples.

Her arrival filled with joy,
with light and harmony, all of Anahuac.

Juan Diego came walking by the mountain
and then came close upon hearing song.

To Juan Diego the Virgin said:
This hill I choose to make my altar.

And in Juan Diego's cloak among painted roses
she chose to leave her beloved image.

—Mexico

REFLECTION: Guadalupe, like many folk stories in the Christian tradition, brings an "outsider" view of what the church is all about. How do you encounter that view today? How is it reflected in the beatitudes of Fr. José Alfredo Goncalves? Meditate on your relationship with the poor. In what ways have you experienced blessing in the encounter? What has most challenged you?

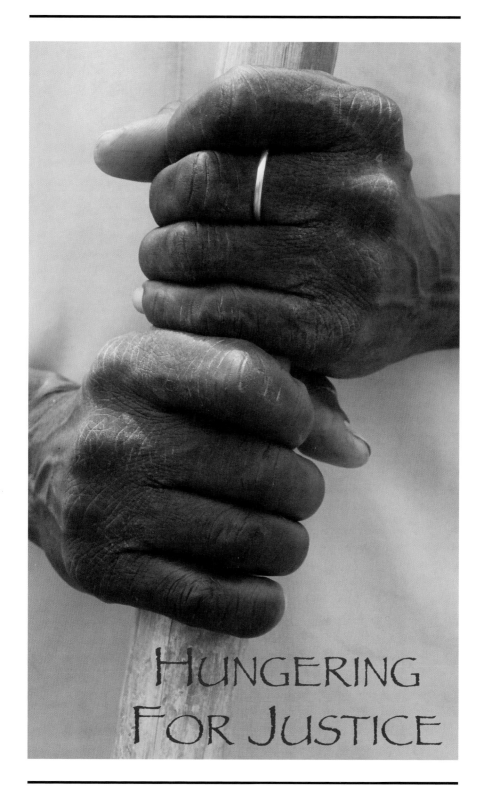

HUNGERING
FOR JUSTICE

To Those Who Are Hungry

God our Creator,
to those who are hungry and thirsty,
give food and drink.

To those who are not hungry and thirsty,
give a hunger and a thirst for justice.

Help us to share in the creation of a more just and peaceful world.

Bless the Lenten alms we set aside in our household
for the good of any sister or brother in need.

We pray through Christ the Lord.

**–Catholic Relief Services
USA**

God the Father, I give you thanks for all the marvels you have created.
I praise you and I bless you for the inestimable grace of life
that you give to us.
Transform me, make me a better Christian,
a living testimony of your mercy and of your power.

Strip me, Lord, of all roots of bitterness,
of false pride and haughtiness of heart.
Make me meek and humble of heart as was our Lord Jesus Christ,
and never let me wound with my words or actions
the dignity of any person.

Put in my heart the ardent desire
to work earnestly for the poor and the needy.
Show me the garment with which you clothed me
the day that I received you as Lord and Savior of my life.
May I wear those garments at the service of my neighbor
and of this community.

Use me, Lord, for your work.

–Ligia de Milla
El Salvador

REFLECTION: Lent is springtime, training time, get-ready-for-Baptism time. The Christian community, the household, and the individual, all are invited to take on the Lenten disciplines of prayer and alms and fasting. What kind of fasting will help you see yourself and the world with gospel clarity this year? What kind of almsgiving will help to make the world more just? What kind of prayer will teach you how to be in the presence of God?

About Catholic Relief Services: The first prayer was written for CRS' Operation Rice Bowl program. With its characteristic cardboard bowl and its opportunities for prayer and action, Operation Rice Bowl has been a Lenten staple in U.S. parishes for nearly 30 years. Millions of Catholics in 170 dioceses in the United States participate by praying, fasting, learning and giving in solidarity with hungry people throughout the world.

Bountiful Harvest

Our Father,
we thank you for the bountiful harvest
of our different plants:
corn, rice, fruits—rambutan, durian, marang.
And the vegetable garden of cabbage, carrots, ginger, onion
and other products that we harvest from our farmlands.

We pour out to you our prayers,
hoping that this harvest will continue until the years to come.

No words can describe how thankful we are
to savor such blessings from you.

Through this, we lift them up all to you,
O most sacred One.

–Edwin Enping
Philippines

I pray to God:
Please let the rain come down
so I can get some water to drink.

I can get some water to give to my rice field
so my rice field will make a good harvest.

Then I will have plenty of full rice bowls
and I will have rice straw to burn for cooking.

—Vietnam

Lord Jesus,
in images of farming and rural life
you announced your gospel to the poor.

We pray for rural men and women,
especially for those who work hard in the fields.

Give us the strength of your Spirit to be witnesses
and collaborators of the creative providence.

May we always sow in ourselves and in our families
the holiness and hope of Christian life,
with the same zeal with which we cultivate our land.

Bless the daily efforts of farmers and farm workers.
Let all recognize the dignity of their labor.

Raise from among us men and women
at the service of the gospel,
sisters and brothers to announce unceasingly
your love for this world that is your own field and farm.

We give you glory forever and ever.

—Fr. Ermolao Portella
Colombia

REFLECTION: During Lent, CRS invites Catholics in the United States to reflect on and respond to world hunger. In what ways is the world God's own "field and farm"? What is God planting in the field that is your community? What is the nature of your labor there?

In My Prayer

In my prayer,
make me a baby girl
who when born is considered to be a burden or curse on the family –
that I may know what it is to feel unwanted.

In my prayer,
make me a girl whose brothers are the only ones sent to school –
that I may understand:
before our creator we are equal; still one is deprived.

In my prayer,
make me a young girl who is not married –
that I may know the fear
of how property will hinder my choice for marriage.

In my prayer,
make me a young girl married in a family exchange –
that I may experience how miserable it is
to marry a person of double or triple my age.

In my prayer,
make me a widow who has no source of earning –
that I may understand:
without any source of income, how can I bring sweets for my children!

In my fast, make me an empty bowl –
that you may fill the hollow space in me with love.

In my almsgiving, make me a grain of rice –
that in the company of others, my gifts may feed a starving world.

O our Lord, give me strength –
that I can share the sadness of my fellow beings
and bring a light of hope for them.

Amen.

—Attique Swati
Pakistan

REFLECTION: Meditate slowly on the women in the stanzas of this prayer by Attique Swati, who works for Catholic Relief Services in Pakistan. Allow yourself to feel the depth of the women's indignities, frustrations, fears and laments. Look out of their eyes as you learn, fast, pray and give this Lent. What do you see!

About Catholic Relief Services: Women and girls are among the most vulnerable members of Pakistani society, facing early childhood marriages, exclusion from schooling, domestic violence, and limited access to health care. In support of the rights of women, CRS assists Pakistani women in starting their own small businesses, promotes education for girls, and helps women overcome social, gender and religious biases.

In Praise Of Generosity

The sun is hot in Tecun Uman –
This town of beginnings and endings.
Dusty and dangerous and filled with possibilities.

In the many bars women become slaves –
To men, to drugs, to violence.
And among these women walk two angels.

Like Jesus they walk with the sinners –
They invite the women to a better life.
They treat them as children of God.

What courage, what love, these two angels –
Their faces radiate beauty, inside and out.
Their love is selfless and joy-filled.

Angels are present in heaven;
Angels are present on earth.
I have seen two Angels in Tecun Uman.

–Andy Zampini, SFO
USA

The man who is truly generous gives to the beggar who approaches him, thin and in search of food. He puts himself at the service of the man who calls to him from the road, and makes him a friend for times to come.

That man is no friend who does not give of his own nourishment to his friend, the companion at his side. Let the friend turn away from him; this is not his dwelling place. Let him find another man who gives freely, even if he be a stranger.

Let the stronger man give to the man whose need is greater; let him gaze upon the lengthening path. For riches roll like the wheels of a chariot, turning from one another.

—The Rig Veda
India

REFLECTION: In some ways the most startling and uncomfortable quality of Jesus during his public ministry was his choice of friends. To follow Jesus meant walking with Jesus' friends as well—women in prostitution, men who collected taxes, people considered physically and ritually unclean. Who do you know who walks comfortably among those whom society does not welcome? What does it mean to be generous with Jesus' friends?

About Catholic Relief Services: The Diocese of Wilmington in Delaware partners with the Diocese of San Marcos in Guatemala through CRS' Global Solidarity Partnerships program, which helps build solidarity among Catholics in the United States and our neighbors overseas through trips and exchanges.

In 2003, Andy Zampini, the director of parish social ministries for the Diocese of Wilmington, visited San Marcos as part of the program. There, the delegation from Wilmington learned firsthand of the experiences of migrants by visiting local outreaches, such as Casa de Mujer, a home for women leaving prostitution, run by the Oblate Sisters.

I f I really had my preference, I would take you to Rwanda to see for yourselves. I was able to stay for four days in a rural village named Gikonko. It is nowhere in a country that is nowhere, and that makes it the perfect place to be. It is like this. The scoutmaster who taught me about geology taught us to look on the other side of rocks. There, you can find things that can otherwise be overlooked.

In America, it is so easy to overlook the human atrocities that have occurred in the world, to overlook AIDS, and the real faces of poverty. To understand these issues, to understand what is going on in the thousands of "nowheres" to which we do not pay attention, we need to look on the other side of the rock.

When I came home and spent $100 on clothes, I stopped. On the other side of the rock, that would have been tuition for almost one year of high school for one youth. Here, the most valuable thing people own is a house; in Rwanda it is a cow.

I know that when you hear stories of the developing world and Rwanda in particular, you may have a sense of empathy, but I hope that you will be open to a relationship of the heart with the people whose stories we tell or others tell. Because that relationship will be transformational in your life, and it will allow you to see the other side of the rock, even if you never get to go.

–David Heimann
USA

REFLECTION: From where you sit, what has been your experience of the "other side of the rock"? What images, stories or experiences move you closer to the world's poor? What conditions foster such a "relationship of the heart," and how can you increase them in your life?

About Catholic Relief Services: David Heimann, a youth minister at St. Ignatius Parish in the Archdiocese of Chicago, visited Rwanda through CRS' "Called to Witness" program in 2003. Developed in partnership with the National Federation of Catholic Youth Ministry, participants visit CRS programming overseas and work with mentors in Catholic youth ministry to integrate their experience into their work with youth.

Without Borders, Without Flags

Where do you come from, where are you going?
I come from all places, I have no name.
I know pain and hunger.
I seek land, home, food,
Life!

Where do you come from, where are you going?
I come from the underground,
Forgotten and dark, fetid and filthy.
I seek dignity and peace, the light of day,
Citizenship!

Where do you come from, where are you going?
I come from the drainage ditch and from abandonment,
I know nostalgia and I lose hope,
I seek gestures of friendship,
Solidarity!

Where do you come from, where are you going?
I come from far and wide:
Black, yellow, white, indigenous.
I am your "other," different,
I am a person!

Where do you come from, where are you going?
I come from discrimination,
From prejudice.
I know walls, laws, fears, loneliness;
I want a world without borders
Or flags!

Where do you come from, where are you going?
I come from the resistance, from the struggle,
From a situation of senselessness,
Valiant and intrepid in the voyage.
Of life I make rhyme and satire
On the way to the Great Homeland!

—Fr. Alfredo José Goncalves
Brazil

Once a rich father took his child on a journey to the countryside with the firm intent that the child see how poor certain people were and understand the value of things and how fortunate their family was. They spent a day and a night in the farmhouse of a very humble peasant family.

Upon concluding the trip, on the way home, the father asked the child, "What did you think of the trip?"

"Very pretty, Dad!"

"Did you see how poor and needy people can be?"

"Yes."

"And what did you learn?"

"I saw that we have a dog at home; they have four. We have a twenty-meter pool; they have a creek without end. We have imported lamps in the patio; they have the stars. Our patio goes to the wall of the house; theirs goes to the horizon. Especially, Dad, I saw that they have time to converse and to live in family. You and mom have to work all of the time and I almost never see you."

The father remained speechless and the child added, "Thank you, Dad, for showing me how rich we could someday be."

—Ecuador

REFLECTION: Solidarity can be imagined as a shared walk, accompanying another in reaching a difficult destination. For the non-poor, a relationship of mutuality, receptivity, and common cause with people who live in poverty can require a complete change in perspective, as the second story suggests. Reflect on the question "Where do I come from and where am I going?" in your call to solidarity with the poor.

The Marks Of The Nails

Creator Spirit, help us respond to your call to be members of one family.
Guide us to constant, peaceful concern
for sisters and brothers throughout the world.
Make us mindful of the needs of those
who must endure day by day the injustice of hunger and poverty.
Bless us all this Lenten season
that we may live in harmony and unity with others.
Renew our Christian commitment to the global family.

–Catholic Relief Services
USA

This is the story of a little boy who had a bad temper. His father gave him a bag of nails and told him that every time that he lost his patience, he should hammer one nail on the back of the door.

The first day the boy hammered 37 nails. In the following days, in the measure that he learned to control his temper, he hammered ever fewer nails. He discovered that it was easier to control himself than hammer nails on the back of the door.

The day arrived in which he could control his temper during the whole day. His father suggested to him that he take a nail out for every day that he was able to control himself.

The days passed and he was able to announce to his father that there were no more nails to remove. The man took him by the hand, led him to the door, and said to him, "You have worked hard, my son, but look at those holes in the wood. It will never be the same. Every time that you lose your patience, you leave wounds like the ones you see here."

–Chile

God in heaven, you have helped my life to grow like a tree.
Now something has happened.
Satan, like a bird, has carried in one twig of his own choosing after another.
Before I knew it he had built a dwelling place and was living in it.
Tonight, my Father, I am throwing out both the bird and the nest.

–Nigeria

*

REFLECTION: Lenten fasting can be fasting from words: hurtful words, gossip words, disparaging words. Such fasting doesn't end with Easter; it shapes a baptized life year-round. This Lent reflect on the nail marks still visible in the wood of your life. What story do they tell you of your own deaths and redemptions!

CELEBRATING

NEW LIFE

We Believe

I will not believe in the law of the strongest,
In the language of guns,
In the power of the powerful.

I want to believe in the rights of all,
In the open hand,
In the strength of the non-violent.

I will not believe in race or riches,
In privileges,
In the established order.

I want to believe that all human beings
Are human beings
And that the order of force and of injustice
Is a disorder.

I will not believe that I don't have to concern myself
With what happens far from here.

I want to believe that the whole world
Is my home, the field that I sow,
And that all reap what all have sown.

I will not believe that I can combat oppression out there
If I tolerate injustice here.

I want to believe that what is right
Is the same here and there
And that I will not be free
While even one human being is excluded.

I will not believe that war and hunger are inevitable
And that peace is inaccessible.

I want to believe in the love of bare hands,
In peace on earth.

I will not believe that any effort is in vain.
I will not believe that the dream of human beings
Continues being only a dream
And that death is the end.

But I dare to believe in the dream of God:
A new heaven, a new earth
Where justice reigns.

–Dom Helder Camara
Brazil

REFLECTION: In the darkness between Holy Saturday and Easter Sunday, Catholics throughout the world gather around the baptismal pool. Those who are prepared and chosen are baptized, and all the church acclaims what is believed and what is renounced. In this creed, Dom Helder does the same thing. Reflect on the ways you have passed over in Christ from death to life this year.

About Catholic Relief Services: Chico Macena, a peasant farmer who lives in Brazil's semi-arid northeast region, has seen new life spring up in the parched area where he lives. With water sources once as far away as 1,000 meters, women spent nearly 50 hours per month just transporting water to their families, he says. With the addition of nearby cisterns, built with the help of CRS, water collection takes only about one hour of labor per month. The time savings alone has greatly increased the well-being of poor families in the region.

Butter In The Milk

One day a young aspirant went to see an old saint who lived beside a river in a small hut made of hemp sacks and bamboo poles. The simple atmosphere of the hut calmed the aspirant's mind and he enjoyed the company of the saint very much. When the time came to leave, the young man asked the saint if he could ask him an important question.

"Of course, my son," said the saint.

"Where can I find God?"

The saint smiled. "That is not an easy question. Allow me to dwell on it. Come again tomorrow and I will answer it. Also, please bring a glass of milk."

The young man agreed and went home, excited that the next day his question would be answered. He thought it odd that the saint requested a glass of milk, but it was a simple request to fulfill, so the next day he returned with the glass of milk.

The saint thanked him for the milk and poured it into his begging bowl. Then he put his fingers in the milk and lifted them up, but when the milk ran through them he frowned and repeated the gesture, with the same result.

The young man watched, perplexed, but remained silent. He wished the saint would finish with his foolishness and get to his question.

The saint began feeling through the milk with his hand, occasionally lifting his hand out and staring in his palm, but when he saw his palm was empty he would return to fishing through the milk.

At last the young man's patience was gone and he said, "Guruji, what are you looking for?"

"I have heard that there is butter in milk," said the saint. "I am searching for the butter."

Before he could stop himself the young man laughed and said, "It is not like that. The butter is not separate from the milk, it is a part of it. You have to convert the milk to yogurt and then churn it to make the butter come out."

"Very good!" said the saint. "I believe you have the answer to your question." And he quaffed the bowl of milk in one long drink. "Now go and churn the milk of your soul until you have found God."

–India

As I walk down dusty roads or
busy concrete boulevards
help me God to take the time to see in the eyes of the other,
to recognize the other, in order to respect.

As I encounter many peoples, many races,
help me to appreciate the hand of the other,
to recognize those hands that create and build, in order to work together.

As my path calls me to various places,
help me to learn to walk together with others on paths that lead to peace,
recognizing that by walking with others, in working together,
we learn to recognize ourself in the other,
to recognize and appreciate our differences.

And begin to recognize what love is about.

—Jennifer Jag Jivan
Pakistan

REFLECTION: How easy is it for you to recognize the face of God in the people that you meet? Who challenges you the most in this regard? How would you "churn the milk of your soul" to help see God in all you encounter?

Now I Go To Sleep

Pasar Ikan is a fish market in Sunda Kelapa harbor, north of Jakarta. In and around Pasar Ikan, you can find hundreds of shanty houses on the bank of the harbor and its many canals. The Pasar Ikan community lives in these small crowded houses. Most of the adults make a living at the fish market selling fish, water or ice.

One day, I attended a funeral service at the nearby graveyard. In the graveyard, there were tens of recently dug holes. It caught my attention that the holes were dug very close to each other.

When the people lowered the coffin into the grave, they had to watch their steps very carefully. Some looked so worried with strained face. I asked spontaneously, "Why are these holes dug so close together?"

I heard one old woman reply softly, "We are poor people. We live in small narrow houses and when we die it is the same." Another women commented, "The world is narrow, and so is the heaven."

That comment struck me. Is that what God really promised to us! I tried to reiterate what Jesus said: "Do not let your hearts be troubled. You have faith in God; have faith also in me. In my Father's house there are many dwelling places. If there were not, would I have told you that I am going to prepare a place for you! And if I go and prepare a place for you, I will come back again and take you to myself, so that where I am you also may be."(John 14:1-3)

These words emphasized what we have to know: Death is not an isolation that cuts all relationships and togetherness between us and Jesus Christ. Death is a journey. We are coming back to the Father's house, and there are many dwelling places that can accommodate all people.

—Andar Ismail
Indonesia

My guardian angel, my sweet company,
do not abandon me by night nor by day.
My guardian angel, humbly I ask you;
help me and free me from all danger.

Four little angels are in my bed,
two at my feet and two at my sides
and the Holy Virgin beside me.
She tells me,
"O beautiful child, sleep and rest.
do not be afraid of anything."

O blessed Saint Monica,
mother of Saint Augustine,
bless my little bed,
because now I go to sleep.

—Mexico

REFLECTION: After a Lent filled with "little deaths" of self-sacrifice and abstinence, Easter promises that death no longer has its sting. It calls for a new sort of life, one dedicated to removing the sting of poverty and injustice from the world. This year, how will you respond to the promise and call of Easter?

About Catholic Relief Services: Bringing interfaith groups together to promote peace is an important part of CRS' work in Indonesia. Before one interfaith prayer service in Yogyakarta, for example, Hindu, Muslim, and Protestant leaders chatted informally. It was February 22, Idul Adha Day, when Muslims remember Abraham's sacrifice. At the same time, Christians were observing the personal sacrifices of Lent, while Hindu leaders found that the celebration resonated with their practice of Panca Yajna, "the five sacrifices." The common theme of sacrifice helped the participants focus on their common work of peace.

Light A Holy Fire

Receive this holy fire.
Make your lives like this fire.
A holy life that is seen.
A life of God that is seen.
A life that has no end.
A life that darkness does not overcome.
May this light of God in you grow.
Light a fire that is worthy of your heads.
Light a fire that is worthy of your children.
Light a fire that is worthy of your fathers.
Light a fire that is worthy of your mothers.
Light a fire that is worthy of God.
Now go in peace.
May the Almighty protect you
today and all days.

—Tanzania

God, you have guided your people
throughout their history.
So now as pilgrim children we turn to you,
searching for your image and for a place to rest.
Like a good friend, Lord,
you are always with the poor.
You make yourself a travel companion
to us wayfarers,
to us the undocumented,
the refugees, the migrants,
pilgrims all who walk toward you.
You call us to be witnesses of your love
and to be examples of our faith
in whatever land receives us.
Lord, may the spirit of Pentecost be renewed.
May all peoples, races and languages be one in communion.

—Mexico

REFLECTION: Pentecost ends the 50 days that began with Easter. The story tells of wind and of flames and of languages galore. Where do we look now for the good news of Jesus done with excitement, with joy! How can we support this and perhaps be caught up in it!

LIVING

IN FAITH

This Day, This Night In Peace

O God, you have let me pass this day in peace,
let me pass the night in peace.

O Lord, who has no lord,
there is no strength but in you.

You alone have no obligation.
Under your hand I pass the night.

You are my mother and my father.

–Kenya

O God, you have let me pass the night in peace,
let me pass the day in peace.

Wherever I may go upon my way
which you made peaceable for me,
O God, lead my steps.

When I have spoken, keep lies away from me.
When I am hungry, keep me from murmuring.
When I am satisfied, keep me from pride.

Calling upon you, I pass the day,
O Lord, who has no lord.

–Kenya

Protect me and my loved ones tonight, O blessed One.
Keep us away from harm and danger.
Let our sleep be peaceful so that we awake in the morning
refreshed in body and mind.

If I have strayed from the true path, may I never do so again.
If I have carelessly hurt someone today, by word or deed,
may I be more mindful the next time.
May my actions reflect your love and compassion.
I shall strive to cleanse my heart from hate and envy,
and live in harmony with all people.
Whatever wrong someone may do to me,
may I be compassionate and forgive
and bear no hatred in my heart.
I shall be grateful for the acts of love and consideration shown to me,
no matter how small they appear to be.
For those I love, and for those who love me,
may this life be a blessing and a source of happiness to all beings.

May we be blessed with good health, strength, peace and happiness.
May my parents, brothers and sisters, teachers, friends and relatives
be well and happy.
May all living beings including my enemies find peace.

−Cambodia

REFLECTION: This week, pray the Kenyan morning and evening prayers by yourself, as a family, or with children. Each evening, take one line from the Buddhist prayers from Cambodia and meditate upon how it was made manifest during the past day. What would it mean to express it more fully in the following day?

About Catholic Relief Services: After two decades of war and civil strife and ten years of fragile peace, Cambodia remains one of the poorest countries in the world. Catholic Relief Services' Thaneakea Phum Cambodia Village Banking program (TPC) seeks to increase the income and quality of life of 40,000 low-income rural women and their families through improved access to financial services. Through community-run village banks, Cambodians receive small loans that allow them to start or expand their own businesses.

Thy Wisdom Is Indeed Great

God, provide me with a patience that will enlighten me,
a heart that will calm me down,
a tongue that will talk about you,
a prayer that will be accepted,
a book to take an oath on,
a wealth earned honestly,
and a paradise deserved.

God, when You are to do something,
You just say "Let it be,"
and it's done.

−Ali Kasum
Macedonia

One day as Nasreddin the Hoca was working in his little garden, he became very warm. Seeing no one about, he slipped off his turban to cool his head a trifle; then he sat down in the pleasant shade of a walnut tree. Now, the Hoca's mind was seldom idle, and while he relaxed for a few minutes in the shade, he meditated upon the great wisdom of Allah. Chancing to note a fine watermelon in the garden, he smiled to himself.

"Now there," said he, "is something I'd have done differently had I been Allah. See that great, lovely watermelon growing on a spindly little vine, and then consider the walnut, a midget nut upon a great and lordly tree. Ah, who can fathom the wisdom of Allah? If I had been arranging matters, I should have given the walnuts to the puny vine, and reserved the watermelons for this magnificent tree." So musing, he nodded for a nap.

Suddenly a walnut fell from the tree and landed with a substantial thump on the top of the Hoca's bald head. Awakened, the Hoca ruefully rubbed the lump which had begun to swell on his scalp. Then an understanding smile spread over his face. In due reverence, he fell to his knees.

"O Allah!" he murmured, "Forgive me my presumption. Thy wisdom is indeed great. Suppose I had been arranging matters? I should just now have been hit upon the head by a watermelon. Ah, Allah, great indeed is thy wisdom!"

—Turkey

REFLECTION: Nasreddin, the celebrated sage of the Middle East, sometimes takes the role of a wise judge, sometimes of a holy fool. In Turkey, stories of Nasreddin, also called the Hoca or Hoja, abound. Consider his insights about the ways of God. In what ways does the ancient spiritual call to privilege the poor, welcome the stranger, and care for the orphaned challenge the "ways of humanity"? In what ways does it challenge you?

I give you thanks, Lord,
for my perfect arms
when so many have suffered mutilation.

For my perfect eyes
when so many cannot see.

For my voice that sings
when so many are reduced to silence.

For my hands that work
when so many beg.

O wondrous Lord,
to have a home, to return to it,
when there are so many brothers and sisters
who have nowhere to go.

To smile, to dream, to love,
when so many cry,
and so many hate each other.

Above all,
to have little to ask you for
and so much to thank you for.

—**Diocese of Juigalpa**
Nicaragua

Someone came to a merchant to tell him that the enclosed marketplace where he had a store had burned down. The merchant panicked and immediately ran to see what happened in the marketplace.

On the way he met a friend who had just been to the marketplace. He said, "Your store alone is standing. It was not caught by the fire, but the other stores have burned down." The merchant exclaimed, "Thank you, God!"

After some time the merchant passed away. One night his son dreamed about him. In the dream the son saw his father suffering and asked him the reason for that.

His father answered, "My son, when people told me that our store didn't burn down, I thanked God as if I didn't care about other people's suffering."

—Ali Kasum
Macedonia

REFLECTION: Upon hearing stories of others' misfortunes, it's not uncommon for people to respond with appreciation for all they themselves have. In the end, however, gratitude is a very humble posture, one that recognizes that what we have never comes solely from our own efforts. Make a list of all that you are grateful for. As you reflect on each item, ask God how you might use that gift in service to others.

About Catholic Relief Services: As the war in the former Yugoslavia threatened to spread south toward Macedonia in the early 1990s, CRS helped local partners to reduce conflict in Macedonia by strengthening the country's economic and social stability. Now, as part of CRS programming, women are running their own small businesses, parents are becoming more involved in the education of their children, and community projects are providing work and bringing people together.

Almighty Creator,
help us see that your plan is not established
until all are allowed to contribute their unique talents.

Help us realize that none of us can move forward
as long as one of us is left behind.

Help us work not in competition for our own gain or purpose,
but rather in cooperation towards fulfillment
of your plan for all of us.

We pray "Thy kingdom come, thy will be done."
And we work towards that.

–John Clossick
USA

Lord, I sing your praise
the whole day through, until the night.

Dad's nets are filled; I have helped him.
We have drawn them in, stamping the rhythm
with our feet, the muscles tense.
We have sung your praise.

On the beach there were our mammies,
who brought the blessings out of the nets,
out of the nets and into their basins.

They rushed to the market, returned, and brought again.
Lord, what a blessing is the sea, with fish in plenty.

Lord, that is the story of your grace:
nets tear and we succumb because we cannot hold them.

Lord, with your praise we drop off to sleep.
Carry us through the night.

Make us fresh for the morning.
Hallelujah for the day!
And blessing for the night!

Amen.

—Ghana

REFLECTION: John Clossick, who works at Bishop Feehan High School in Attelboro, Massachusetts, traveled to Ghana as part of CRS' Frontiers of Justice Program. The preceding prayers—one traditional to Ghana and the other the product of Clossick's visit there—share a vision of the common good. How does this vision resonate with your life? In what ways has God filled your net to overflowing? How are you called to use the contents?

MAKING ROOM
FOR PEACE

Bearing Witness To Peace

Lord God, we come to you in our need.
Create in us an awareness of the massive forces
that threaten our world today.
Give us a sense of urgency
to activate the forces of goodness, of justice, of love and of peace.

Where there is armed conflict,
let us stretch our arms to our brothers and sisters.
Where there is abundance,
let there be simple lifestyle and sharing.

Where there is poverty,
let there be dignified living and constant striving for just structures.
Where there are wounds of division,
let there be unity and wholeness.
Help us to be committed to the building of your kingdom.

Not seeking to be cared for,
but to care.
Not expecting to be served,
but to place ourselves in the service of others.
Not aspiring to be materially secure,
but to place our security in your love.

Teach us your spirit.
Only in loving imitation of you
can we discover the healing springs of life
that will bring new birth to our world.

–Philippines

O almighty One who created everything,
you are witness to the sincerity of each one in this circle.

O you trees who have been here since time immemorial,
as proven by your thick trunk and deep roots,
you bear silent witness to the words spoken here today.

O you stones who have been here for centuries,
we believe that you have grown from dust to pebbles to stones
through hundreds of years.
You are witness to the stories and tears that have unfolded here today.

You winds who blow gently around us,
you fan our bodies and souls with your gentle breeze.
Cool our anger
and let the realities brought out here remain within this circle
and not be blown and scattered all around the land
until the proper time.

—East Timor

REFLECTION: The act of reconciliation in countries that have known ongoing and devastating conflict requires people to have the space to tell their stories and to remember what is often too painful to speak of but too important to forget. Pray for the people in your community who have emigrated from places of conflict and pain. Seek out opportunities to learn their stories; look for ways to help them feel welcome, listened to, and cared for.

About Catholic Relief Services: After 450 years of foreign rule, East Timor became the world's newest nation with its independence in May 2002. CRS is assisting the East Timorese people in their efforts to build a democratic and more peaceful society by providing training in conflict resolution, mediation and peaceful communication, and supporting local church partners in their work to foster reconciliation, human rights and peace.

Strength

The animals had begun bickering about who was the strongest, so they decided to settle the matter with a contest.

Chimpanzee was the first to step forward. "This is strength!" he cried as he pulled over a small sapling with his long, strong arms and proceeded to tie it in a knot.

Indeed, agreed the animals, that was strength!

Deer leapt up next. "Witness my strength!" she called with a toss of her slender neck. Her voice trailed out behind her as she sprang through the forest, returning soon after with the sprig of a tree that grew several miles from the place. She hadn't even broken a sweat.

Indeed, agreed the animals, that was strength!

Leopard followed. "I'll show you strength," he said drawing out his long, sharp claws one by one. Then he attacked the ground with a fury, tossing up dust and dirt as he fashioned an impressive hole.

Indeed, agreed the animals, that was strength!

At last it was elephant's turn. With thundering steps she lumbered to the end of a row of great trees and, putting her shoulder to the nearest one, she leaned against it. Immediately, it toppled into its neighbor, which caused the chain of great trees to crash to the ground one by one, echoing through the jungle for miles.

Elephant didn't need to say a word. Indeed, agreed the animals, that was strength!

Now Human had arrived late to the contest, having first stopped to hide something in the bushes nearby.

"You cannot decide upon a winner until you have seen what I can do!" Human announced.

Stepping into the center of the circle of animals, Human sprang into the air and began to leap and whirl, turning handsprings and cartwheels and summersaults.

"Hey, strength!" Human cried with a flourish at the end of the routine.

But the animals did not agree.

"Well, human that was clever, and indeed you seem quite winded. But was that strength? What else can you do?"

Human was a bit put out, but offered another display. Scampering quickly up the nearest tree, Human began to toss down great quantities of nuts until they formed a considerable pile on the ground.

"Now, wasn't that strength?" Human demanded, hopping down from the tree.

"Does it take strength to climb a tree?" inquired the animals. "There must be something else you can do."

At that Human ran to his bush, and pulled out a long object of wood and metal. It was the first gun.

"Now," Human cried, pointing the gun right at Elephant. "Feel my strength."

With a loud crack, and a flash and a burst of smoke, the gun went off. Elephant slowly, slowly sank to the ground and did not move again.

"Aha! Aha!" cried Human. "I have defeated the strongest one of all! You must name me the victor!"

But when the echo of Human's shouts subsided, Human was alone. All of the animals had fled.

Later the animals huddled in the darkest part of the forest. They wept for the loss of their friend, Elephant, and whispered in frightened voices of what had happened.

From that day on, they agreed, they would never walk with or speak with Human again. For Human is the only creature in the forest who does not know the difference between strength and death.

—West Africa

REFLECTION: In a globalized world, strength—both military and economic—is a value that is tightly held. Yet the gospel offers an alternate view, one in which strength is found among the weak, where winning only comes by losing all, and where as Mary says in her Magnificat, the lowly are raised to high places. Reflect upon these contrasting views of strength. How do they affect your actions and the choices you make?

Peace In Colombia

Lord Jesus Christ,
make us instruments of your peace.
Where there is hatred, let us sow love.
Where there is injury, let us offer pardon.
Where there is discord, let us build peace.

Oh divine Lord, you taught us that those who work for peace
are called the children of God.
Help us to persist in establishing justice and truth
as firm and lasting foundations of peace.

Lord, you offer us peace as a gift
and peace as a responsibility that we must realize with your help.
Give us the grace to reach out for peace,
to have attitudes of peace,
that our words may be words of peace,
and our works be works of peace.
Then may we build the peace that we and our nations need.

**–Monseñor Pedro Rubiano Sáenz,
Cardinal of Colombia and Archbishop of Bogotá**

For brothers and sisters whose human rights are being violated...
Hear our prayer, O Lord.

For the implantation in Colombia of justice
based on the full recognition of human rights...

For every person in authority who respects and cares
for and protects the lives of all Colombians...

For those who show attitudes of fellowship, tolerance,
reconciliation, solidarity, dialogue and justice...

For those who participate in the search for peace and in building peace through
commitment to the good of all our brothers and sisters...

For those who have died by violent acts and the denial of human rights...

For all who practice devotion to St. Pedro Claver...

**–Caritas
Colombia**

REFLECTION: Saint Peter Claver, a seventeenth-century Spanish priest, is remembered for his dedication to defending the dignity and the rights of black slaves and marginalized ethnic groups in Colombia. The Colombian Congress in 1985 proclaimed September 9, the feast of Saint Peter Claver, as the "Colombian Day of Human Rights." It falls during the week when people throughout Colombia call for peace, justice, respect and human rights as part of "Semana por la paz" (week for peace). The Social Ministry office of the Colombian Bishop's Conference encourages Catholics in the United States to join them in this week for peace by holding their own solidarity events.

About Catholic Relief Services: In what has been called the worst humanitarian crisis in the Americas, conflict in Colombia has claimed nearly 40,000 lives in the past decade and displaced nearly three million people since 1985. CRS' In Solidarity with Colombia program pursues opportunities to increase solidarity and promote a more just policy toward Colombia. CRS also provides emergency and humanitarian assistance and supports local efforts in peace and human rights education and reconciliation.

How Do You Explain?

How do you explain peace to a child born in war?
How do you talk about trust when hatred is all she knows?
How do you talk about RIGHTS when WRONGS abound?
How do you describe tomorrow, when today is such is mess?

How do you describe joy to an embittered child,
a child accustomed to unparalleled horror and hate?
How do you describe a home to a child living in war
when life in temporary camps is so routine and real?

What do you say about having a family in the midst of chaos,
when the family he knows are his abusers and users?
When do you tell her about respect and love,
when slavery and sex are the reasons she is kept alive?

What do you say about life and its attendant joy,
when body counts are the only joys he is taught to share?
What do you tell him about school, play and work
amidst the heartless carnage and devastation around?

How can you describe trust
when trusting no one is a matter of must?
What you do say about friendship
when the best friend he has is the weapon he carries?

What do you tell her about hope
when all her life feels like sliding down a slope?
How do you tell her she is a child, a beautiful child,
when her beauty and age have brought her so much pain?

How do you talk about peace, joy, hope or love?
What do you say about RIGHTS, friendship or family?
How do you talk about life, school, play or work?

How do you talk about peace
to a child born in war?

—Saah Charles N'Tow
Liberia

Sunday will come again.
These deserted streets will come alive.

Laughter of children and parents will fill the air.
Fear will fade and joy will gradually return.

The church bell will ring again.
The pews will be full again.

People will serve in joyful obedience.
People will dance and sing praises to our God.

Sunday will come again.
Sunday will come again.

When cries of anguish will no longer be heard
And death will find a place elsewhere.

–Saah Charles N'Tow
Liberia

REFLECTION: Saah Charles N'Tow is a Liberian national, peace activist and poet who fled the civil war in his native country in the early 1990s. He lived as a refugee in Sierra Leone, Ghana, and Europe and has worked with refugee youth in the United Kingdom and the United States. He now lives in Rhode Island. In these poems, N'Tow asks a question that every parent must face: How do you talk about peace to a child? Consider the ways that children in the United States learn about and experience war and violence. How do you talk with children about peace?

About Catholic Relief Services: Since Liberia's civil war began in 1989, more than 1 million people have been displaced by violent conflict. While the country now steps toward peace, CRS is working to assist those who have been uprooted from their homes with emergency food and medical assistance. CRS has been working in Liberia since 1990 on issues ranging from justice and reconciliation to agriculture, health care and education.

FOSTERING
WHOLENESS

AND DIGNITY

A Potter Shaping The Clay

✔ We believe that we are part of God's dream for the church and the world,
and that God is shaping us, as the potter shapes the clay,
into the kind of human and church community
that is the dream in God's heart.

✔ We believe that God has called and chosen us
as the potter carefully chooses a lump of clay
to make what the potter has in mind.

✔ We believe that when God sees that the church and the world
are not coming out right, not according to the divine dream,
God does not discard the clay and take another piece,
but reworks the same clay, shaping and molding it
with firm but gentle hands, on the wheel of life.

We believe that God is shaping and reshaping us
through our response to the AIDS pandemic
to be like Jesus, the compassionate one,
as we continue the mission of Jesus in the world.

✔ We confess that we sometimes become discouraged and disheartened
with the weight of people's suffering.

✔ We confess that we sometimes grow weary
and forget that God is with us when we feel overwhelmed
by the enormity of people's pain,
their grinding poverty, their desperation.

✔ We confess that we sometimes forget
that God does provide and our needs will be met.

We confess that our faith in humanity is shaken
when people with AIDS feel abandoned and judged
and are treated as outcasts.

✔ We commit ourselves to being gentle
with the crushed reed, the wavering flame,
so that the crushed reed will not be broken
nor the flickering flame quenched.

We commit ourselves to healing, helping and educating
so that the AIDS pandemic will be overcome in Southern Africa.
We will do what we can for the orphans
and for others whose lives are bent or broken by AIDS.

We commit ourselves to shaping with gentle hands
the fragile and vulnerable clay, each precious person given to us.
We will treat them with the same loving patience we ourselves feel
in the hands of the divine potter.
We will open our ears to listen like disciples
as God leads us forward on the next part of the journey,
the journey we are on together.
And we will join hands as we continue along the way,
the way of salvation. *Amen*

–AIDS Office
Southern African Conference of Catholic Bishops

REFLECTION: How is God reshaping us through our response to HIV/AIDS in Africa and the world? Make a point of marking World AIDS Day, December 1, on your calendar, as a time to learn more about global AIDS. Pray for those affected and advocate for ways that the United States government can help address the pandemic.

About Catholic Relief Services: In 2004, CRS' HIV/AIDS programs served approximately two million people affected by HIV/AIDS in 31 countries in Africa, Asia and Latin America. In addition to providing direct care for people with AIDS, CRS helps to educate and empower community members so that they can care for the ill and the orphaned, counsel and teach one another how to avoid the disease, and strengthen their ability to overcome the economic and social affects of the disease.

Faith In Our Bodies

Father, thank you for your revelation
about death
and illness
and sorrow.

Thank you for speaking so plainly to us,
for calling us all friends
and hovering over us;
for extending your arms out to us.

We cannot stand on our own;
we fall into death without you.
We fall from faith, left to our own.
We are really friendless without you.

Your extended arms fill us with joy,
expressing love,
love caring and carrying,
asking and receiving our trust.

You have our trust, Father,
and our faith,
with our bodies
and all that we are and possess.

We fear nothing when with you,
safe to stretch out and help others,
those troubled in faith,
those troubled in body.

Father, help us to do with our bodies what we proclaim,
that our faith be known to you
and to others,
and be effective in all the world.

—Tanzania

God of the poor,
AIDS does not discriminate by race or religion or economic class.
But people do.
Help us respond to the cry of the poor for AIDS medications,
for health care, for food, for education, for communities of support.

God of compassion,
Help us to step toward our sisters and brothers who have AIDS,
those who are an ocean away and those in our own communities.
Stand with us in solidarity beside them.

God of the orphans,
in Africa you see the children of those who have died of AIDS.
Call us all to a global village
to raise these children in love and hope.

—Catholic Relief Services
USA

REFLECTION: Consider for a moment what would happen to your community if all the people between the ages of 15 and 60 were removed! What would happen to the young and to the old! What would happen to systems of education, commerce, government and health care! This has been the legacy of HIV/AIDS in many parts of the world. When you pray for the more than 8,500 people who die of AIDS each day, pray also for the people who remain. You are one of them. How are you called to respond!

Seventeen Syllables

As I went from person to person and place to place during a two-week visit to CRS programming in Tanzania and Ethiopia, I had difficulty writing it all down. To capture the essence of what I experienced, I translated my notes into haiku, the 17-syllable Japanese poetry form:

VISITING MATATA FRANCIS
In Kiswahili
His name translates to "problems,"
AIDS, the latest one.

PASADA AIDS PROGRAM
When women return
To learn the AIDS test results
Their futures come too.

JUST A NORMAL LIFE
Just a normal life.
Known only to her mother,
AIDS is her secret.

KISORYA CHOIR
Like a Greek chorus
The young sing of HIV
To halt tragedy.

MISSIONARIES OF CHARITY HOME
Hope leads to healing
When patients know they are loved.
Touch is medicine.

–Barbara Ballenger
USA

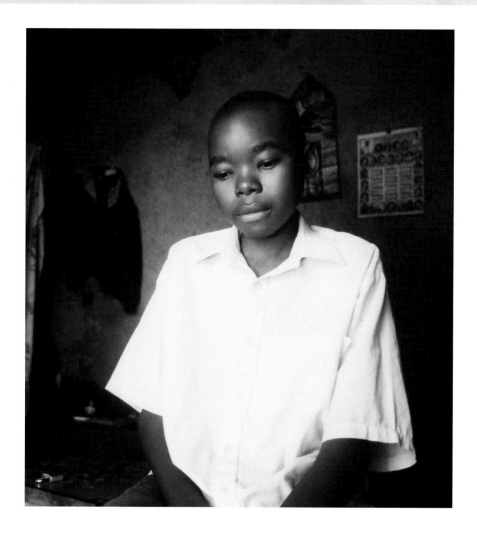

REFLECTION: Haiku requires a first line of five syllables, a second line of seven syllables, and a third line of five syllables. Reflect upon recent moments of awareness in your relationship with people and God. Use the haiku form to get at the heart of what you have experienced.

Africa, O Africa!

Our land of Africa, what should we do?
Africa, O Africa, our land of Africa.

Africa, why Africa?
Africa is on the mouth every day.
Africa has got so many problems here and there.
Africa is crying every day.
Why Africa?

Our land of Africa, what should we do?
Africa, O Africa, our land of Africa.

Look at our brothers and sisters
who are in northern Uganda.
Why are they dying?

Our land of Africa, what should we do?
Africa, O Africa, our land of Africa.

My mother and father also,
my beloved brothers.
They are nowhere to be seen.

Our land of Africa, what should we do?
Africa, O Africa, our land of Africa.

I am an orphan who doesn't have anybody.
Who can look after me?
O Africa!

Our land of Africa, what should we do?
Africa, O Africa! Our land of Africa.

—**Alberto Bisaso**
Uganda

The Magama Center (a school for orphans in central Zimbabwe) reminded me of Bertrandville (Louisiana), which, growing up, was the definition of country to me, a city kid from New Orleans. It reminded me of my mother's church, St. Benedict the Moor, with the church hall, the church, and kids playing in the yard. The surrounding community where people live—"up and down the lanes," as we called it—it reminded me of that, too, and of kids playing in the sugar cane fields in Louisiana. At Magama, I was reminded of what a Saturday afternoon growing up would be like. Go out and play, but there's work to do before that.

It wasn't until I thought about the fact that we were there because people are dying, almost like something was happening behind the curtain—death—something else was going on there, that I was reminded of what's left, all the humanity that needs to be taken care of.

Recently at home, I was watching the tape of Mandelo, one child late in the afternoon of the presentation, who could not hold back her pain when she had to sing, "I am an orphan." That was the defining moment; how many kids are left behind. It is so horrible that this is happening when something could be done, and it's happening right before us.

People always look back at events from the past and ask what more they could have done when it was happening. This is one of those moments in our time where we are going to be judged by what we do now.

—Wendell Pierce
USA

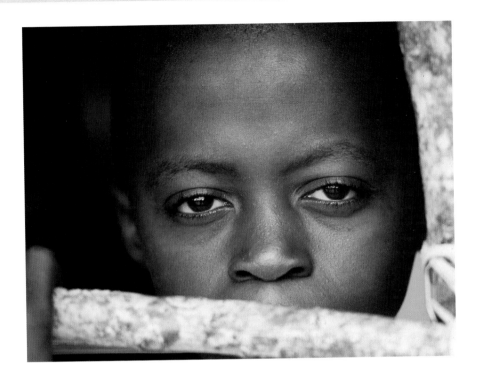

(J

REFLECTION: In Africa, where more than 11 million children have been left orphaned by AIDS, choirs of children often write and sing about their experiences and warn of the consequences of the disease. Wendell Pierce notes the pain of Mandelo, a child who had lost her mother just three days before, as she sings of the suffering of orphans. Her words echo the message of the children of Kampala, Uganda as they sing "Africa O Africa." Consider this instance of solidarity among the children of Africa. What is the message for you?

About Catholic Relief Services: In November of 2003, actor Wendell Pierce from the Baltimore-based HBO television series, "The Wire," traveled to Zimbabwe with CRS staff to visit HIV/AIDS programs. In an interview with CRS, Pierce discussed his visit to the Magama Life Center in central Zimbabwe, where nearly 800 children, approximately 400 of whom are either AIDS orphans or economically destitute, attend primary school. Pierce also visited the Chinotimba primary school outside Victoria Falls, where he heard Mandelo perform with other members of a "kids club" of orphans and other vulnerable children.

It Is Good To Be Alive

Oh God, we take time to pause from daily work to gather our thoughts;
to let our souls catch up with our bodies;
to feel your presence in your creation;
to ask forgiveness for our lapses, ours and on behalf of your people;
and to be ourselves restored.

Breathing in, God's Spirit calms my body;
breathing out, it's good to be alive.

Lord Jesus Christ, we take time to gather around you.
By your life and teachings may we find our strength,
and journeying together may we find our rest.

Breathing in, Christ lives in our lives;
breathing out, it's good to be alive.

Holy Spirit, creative energy of love and compassion,
life embracing, life transforming,
heal our bodies, heal our souls, heal our relationships, heal our nations.

Breathing in, the Spirit heals;
breathing out, it's good to be alive.

Amen.

–Cora Tabing-Reyes
Christian Conference of Asia

REFLECTION: This invitation to "let our souls catch up with our bodies" is essential in the work of social change. As a way of centering yourself during the day, choose one of the two-line "breath prayers" in this reflection, such as "Breathing in, God's Spirit calms my body. Breathing out, it's good to be alive." As you breath in slowly and rhythmically, say the first line to yourself; as you breath out, say the second.

About Catholic Relief Services: Cora Tabing-Reyes' beautiful prayer was printed in the Asian Centre for the Progress of People's Justice and Peace Bulletin, which provides updates and resources on peace and human rights throughout Asia. Catholic Relief Services collaborates with the centre in its work supporting peace and justice efforts in Asia.

WALKING
IN SOLIDARITY

Shouting Tales Of The Ancient

O mighty Africa, O Ghana,
"Akwaaba!" I am welcome
And God speaks to my soul!

Shouting tales of the ancient,
Woven into a new dance
Of longing, hoping, living!

Amazing with beauty and splendor,
Wide wonder of children
And intimacy between mother and child.

Haunting with the stares of distrust,
The sweat of labor, drudgery,
And the brutal assault of poverty, oppression.

Reaching nonetheless for unity,
Calling for solidarity:
"I want to take you as a friend."

Overflowing with love,
Inviting to the sacrifice, selflessness,
Surrender to love.

Overwhelming with God,
Suffering, despair, crucifixion, death,
Hope, joy, dance, resurrection.

O mighty Africa, O Ghana,
"Akwaaba!" I welcome you!
And God speaks to my soul!

–Ted Miles
USA

REFLECTION: Ted Miles, director of student development at Cardinal Gibbons High School in Baltimore, traveled to Ghana in 2001 as part of CRS' Frontiers of Justice program. How do the images of Africa that he shares in his prayer compare with the images of Africa that are commonly reported in the popular and news media? What images of this prayer resonate most with you? What challenges you the most?

About Catholic Relief Services: At Dr. David Abdulai's Sheikhinah clinic in Tamale, Ghana, the poor receive a generous dose of unconditional love. In addition to free health care, people who are abandoned find a welcoming home, people suffering from HIV/AIDS receive treatment and acceptance, and the dying have a hospice in which they can live out their lives with dignity. Founded in 1991 by Dr. Abdulai, a medical doctor from Tamale, the clinic has been working with CRS/Ghana since 1999.

The Sound Of Justice

One day as Nasreddin the Hoca was walking through the forest, he came upon a peasant cutting wood. It was hard, heavy work, and every blow of the ax on the wood took all the force the peasant could muster. As the Hoca watched, he heard someone saying "Hunh!" every time the ax came down on the wood. There on a log sat the woodcutter's companion. And faithfully, with every blow, he said "Hunh!" The Hoca wondered at this, but he went on his way without saying anything.

In a few days, the peasant went to the bazaar with his load of wood and sold it for a fair sum in coins. As he slipped the sack of coins into the pocket of his baggy trousers, his companion rushed up. "Half of that money is mine!" he insisted. "I did half of the work."

Astonished, the woodcutter debated the matter. Clearly, this was a case to be brought before the judge. Accordingly, the two went before the Hoca, who served the village as judge. Carefully the Hoca listened to both sides of the case. Then, calling the woodcutter to him, he directed him to lay the bag of coins on the stone. One by one, the Hoca dropped the coins on the stone. As they rang out with a pleasant jingle, he said to the companion, "Do you hear this?"

"Yes," the companion answered.

"Fine," said the Hoca. "The sound is yours, and the coin is the woodcutter's."

When the coins had all been sounded and turned over to the woodcutter, the Hoca dismissed the case.

—Turkey

REFLECTION: Consider for a moment the hard, physical labor that goes into providing the goods and services that we often take for granted. Who builds the infrastructure, repairs the roads, cleans the buildings, stocks the shelves, plants and harvests the food, makes the clothes? Who tends to be compensated more, those who do the hardest physical work, or those who oversee them? Make a special effort to notice, greet and pray for those whose physical labor contributes so much to our well-being.

These are the mornings sung about by David the King!
Today, because it is your saint's day, we sing to you here.

Wake up, my love, wake up!
Look, the day has already dawned.
Already the birds are singing.
The moon has already hidden.
How pretty is the morning today when I come to greet you.

We come all with delight and pleasure to congratulate you!
The day that you were born all the flowers were born.
In the baptismal font sang the nightingales.

The light that God gave is already dawning.
Get up this morning and look: It is already dawn!
From all the stars of heaven I have to bring two:
One to greet you, the other to say to you goodbye.

Today, because it is your saint's day, we desire your happiness.
With clusters of flowers I come to greet you.
And today, because it is your saint's day, we come to sing to you.

—Mexico

REFLECTION: In many cultures, acts of solidarity with one's ancestors are woven into the fabric of daily life. In Mexico, where people are often named for Catholic saints, this early morning song is for singing on the feast day of one's saint. Who are you named for? What is that person's feast day or birthday? Pray this prayer on a day that honors a saint, ancestor, or other role model whose name you share.

The Gift Of Work

Thank you, Lord, for permitting me to live this new day!
Thank you all the more for permitting me to begin this workday.

I ask you, Lord, to give me the strength of your blessing:
to share efforts with my fellow workers,
to recognize my mistakes,
and, this very day, to amend
whatever could hamper my work of tomorrow,
be it alone or in collective responsibilities.

I ask you, my Lord, to be the worker here
and, by means of my work instruments,
prepare for the magnificence of your return,
with the harmony of duty fulfilled,
with patience in the midst of impatience,
with community in the face of contempt,
with joy where there has been sadness.

I ask you, Lord, for work for those who do not have it,
for strength of will in all your children
so that they can share this blessing.
In turn, Lord, I offer you little:
simply each moment of this day as it comes.

Let us be your sons and your daughters,
with our heads held high in material work,
and, afterwards, let us prepare to rest in your embrace
and await the coming of a new day to glorify you:
today, tomorrow and always, until our lives be your life.

—Caritas
Nicaragua

Father, I give you thanks
because you have allowed me to conclude this workday.

How I would love to find myself with my family.
But—you see—the distance does not allow me.

Jesus, you are meek and humble of heart.
Accept the desires and the actions of the day
that I have finished.

Allow me to rest now.
Then with my body and my spirit renewed
I can carry out my work
on behalf of my brothers and sisters.

If in this day I have done some good,
let it be for your greater glory.
If, on the contrary, I have done wrong,
have mercy on me.

—Mexico

REFLECTION: You can support the dignity of workers through the economic choices that you make. The purchase of fair-trade coffee helps small coffee growers who struggle against market forces beyond their control. Buying craft items from organizations such as CRS' partner, SERRV International, supports people who are escaping poverty by forming small worker-run cooperatives.

About Catholic Relief Services: In recent years, coffee retailers in the United States have been enjoying a gourmet coffee boom, while coffee farmers in places like Nicaragua are going bust. Coffee prices have fallen to their lowest level, in real terms, in 100 years, meaning that revenues for small-scale coffee farmers are often lower than the cost of production. CRS has responded in two ways. In Nicaragua, CRS has provided emergency food relief to small-scale coffee farmers, as well as technical assistance in quality control and marketing. In the United States, CRS is promoting the purchase of Fair Trade Certified coffee, which ensures that coffee farmers get a fair price for their product.

Time Will Tell

, Hallelujah!
ɤ Blessed is the work that incarnates the way of Jesus,
the son of the carpenter.

Blessed are those who promote justice with enthusiasm.
Their organization will be a bastion
and their struggle for human rights will be blessed.
In their homes will be tenderness and vigor in abundance.
Their solidarity can always be counted on.

Blessed are those workers who share their bread with the hungry
and, in the manner of Jesus, raise up those bowed down.
They will never vacillate
and the memory of their goodness lives forever.

Blessed are those workers who watch over the lives of their companions
and, in the way of Jesus, expel the demons that attack them.
They will never waver
and trust in them will be perpetual.

They will not be afraid of adversities;
they will live forever, firm and confident in Jesus.
Their spirit will remain unbreakable, without fear,
until they see the retreat of their enemies.
They announce to their companions the Good News,
their joy consists in the defense of their dignity.
Therefore, they will raise their heads at every hour.

(Based on Psalm 112)

**–Cristina Auerbach Benavides
and Carlos G. Rodríguez Rivera, SJ
Mexico**

Once upon a time, there was a little boy who was very naughty and lazy for learning. His parents were very sad about this. One day, when he was playing along a canal, he saw an old woman holding an iron rod and sharpening it against a large rock. He approached the woman but she did not notice. He was so surprised at what the woman was doing that he asked, "Hello! What are you doing?"

The woman replied without looking up as she continued sharpening the iron rod, "You know, little boy, I want to make a needle out of the iron rod."

The little boy was even more surprised and asked the woman, "The iron rod is so big. How can you make a needle out of it!"

"If today I cannot make a needle, then I continue sharpening it tomorrow. The iron rod is indeed so big, but the longer you sharpen it, the smaller it will become. In the end, it will become a needle," replied the old woman.

The boy discovered that whatever we do, it requires patience and no matter how difficult the work is, if we have persistence, we will succeed in the end.

—Vietnam

REFLECTION: Since the nineteenth century, the Roman Catholic Church has been a strong advocate of workers. In what ways does your work "incarnate the way of Jesus!" What does the story of sharpening the iron rod say about the work of peace and justice that Christians are called to pursue throughout the world?

About Catholic Relief Services: In addition to humanitarian relief and economic development, CRS supports people who live in poverty as they address the root causes of injustice, violence, and economic instability in their communities. In the United States, CRS advocates for legislation that addresses the needs of the world's poor, from increasing federal funding for the fight against global HIV/AIDS to seeking policies that promote peace.

INDEX

Index

ᴖ

ACKNOWLEDGMENTS

Published Sources

Page 8
"The Light Prayer of the Prophet Muhammad" from **Women of Sufism, A Hidden Treasure** by Camille Adams Helminski. Boston: Shambhala Publications, Inc., 2003. Reprinted by permission of the author.

Page 10
"The Lion's Whisker" from **Doorways to the Soul: 52 Wisdom Tales from Around the World**, by Elisa Davy Pearmain. The Pilgrim Press, Cleveland, 1998. Reprinted by permission of the publisher.

Page 12
Text 1, "Presence on the Way" from **Companions of Hope: Prayers for Migrant Youth**, published by the Youth and Migration Program of the Mexican Episcopal Commission of Youth Ministry.

Page 19
From **The Road To Bethlehem, A Nativity Story from Ethiopia**, by Elizabeth Laird. London: MacMillan Education LTD, 2000. Reprinted by permission of the publisher.

Page 35
From **The Rig Veda, An Anthology. One hundred and Eight Hymns**, selected translated and annotated by Wendy Doniger O'Flaherty. Penguin Book Ltd., England, 1981. Reprinted by permission of the publisher.

Page 39
"Fortunes of the Country Side, " from **La Culpa Es De La Vaca**, compiled by Jaime Lopera G. and Marta Inés Bernal Trujillo. Bogata: Interval Publishing, 2002. Reprinted by permission of the publisher.

Page 41
Text 1, "The Mark of the Nails, " ibid.

Page 41
Text 2, "You Have Helped My Life to Grow Like A Tree, " from **An African Prayer Book**, by Desmond Tutu. New York: Doubleday, 1995. Reprinted by permission of the publisher.

Page 46

"The Butter in the Milk," from **The Monkeys and the Mango Tree: Teaching Stories of the Saints and Sadhus of India** by Harish Johari. Rochester, VT: Inner Traditions International, 1998. By permission of the publisher.

Page 48

"Di rumah Bapaku Banyak Tempat Tinggal" ("There are Many Dwelling Places in my Father's House") from **Selamat Mengikut Dia: 33 Renungan Tentang Kristus (Let's Follow Him: 33 Reflections about Jesus Christ)** by Dr. Andar Ismail. BPK Gunung Mulia, 1994.

Page 51

Text 1, "Light a Holy Fire, " from **An African Prayer Book**, by Desmond Tutu. New York: Doubleday, 1995. Reprinted by permission of the publisher.

Page 51

Text 2, "The Wayfarer's Prayer" from **Companion of Hopes: Prayers for Migrant Youth**, published by the Youth and Migration Program of the Mexican Episcopal Commission of Youth Ministry.

Page 54

Texts 1 and 2, "An Evening Prayer" and "A Morning Prayer," from **An African Prayer Book**, by Desmond Tutu. New York: Doubleday, 1995. Reprinted by permission of the publisher.

Page 55

Buddhist prayers from **Daily Buddhist Devotions**, by Venerable Sri Dhammananda. Buddhist missionary Society, Kuala Lumpur, Malaysia. First and Second edition 1991 & 1993.

Page 57

"Watermelons, Walnuts, and the Wisdom of Allah" from **Watermelons, Walnuts and the Wisdom of Allah and Other Tales of the Hoca** by Barbara K. Walker. Lubbock: Texas Tech University Press, 1991. Reprinted by permission of the author.

Page 64

"A Fisherman's Song of Praise" from **An African Prayer Book**, by Desmond Tutu. New York: Doubleday, 1995. Reprinted by permission of the publisher.

Page 70
"Strength" from **Peace Tales: World Folktales to Talk About** by Margaret Read MacDonald. New Haven: Linnet Books, 1992. Rewritten by Barbara Ballenger with permission of the author.

Page 82
"You Have Our Faith With Our Bodies" from **An African Prayer Book**, by Desmond Tutu. New York: Doubleday, 1995. Reprinted by permission of the publisher.

Page 96
"The Sound is Yours" from **Watermelons, Walnuts and the Wisdom of Allah and Other Tales of the Hoca** by Barbara K. Walker. Lubbock: Texas Tech University Press, 1991. Reprinted by permission of the author.

Page 102
"They will Live Forever," from **De la Tragedia a la Esperanza: Los Salmos de los Trabajadores**, by Christina Auerbach Benavides and Carlos G. Rodríguez Rivera, SJ. CEREAL Integra. Reprinted by permission of the authors.

(

Photos

All photos by David Snyder unless otherwise indicated.

Cover
    Jerusalem, West Bank

Title Page
    Bhuj, India

Page 5
    Jerusalem, West Bank

Page 6
    Cairo, Egypt - Sudanese refugee learns English (Sakakini Vocational Training CenTer.)

Page 8
    Pela, Jordan

Page 11
    Meta, Ethiopia - woman at home after receiving food at a distribution

Page 15
    Meki, Ethiopia - local family with several malnourished children

Page 16
    El Espino, El Salvador - rural family with 8-year old daughter
        by Richard Lord

Page 22
    Wadi Rum, Jordan

Page 27
    Ouagadugu, Burkina Faso

Page 28
    Yogyakarta, Indonesia - Muning village

Page 30
    Bhuj, India

Page 33
    Bujumbura, Burundi

Page 34
    San Juan Saquatepequez, Guatemala - woman and children carry firewood
        by Sean Sprague

(

Special Thanks

Prayer Without Borders, Celebrating Global Wisdom represents the work of so many people that any list of those who deserve thanks will surely be incomplete. Catholic Relief Services staff, partners, supporters and friends searched out texts that were representative of their regions, tracked down sources and secured permissions. We could not include every text that we received, but our gratitude remains for all who contributed to this project.

The following have my special thanks: Joan Neal, CRS vice president for U.S. Operations, called the idea into reality. Gabe Huck helped shape and edit the book. Dave Snyder and Karen Starr Adams brought their artistry to the pages. Theresa Brown, Kathy Brown, Kevin Whorton, Paul Tillman, Steve Shepherd, Jeff Baeuerlein and Brian Backe lent their guidance. Nerenda Eid offered her marketing skills. Rowena Gono and Barbara Joyner provided editorial assistance. Karen Smith, Michele Gilfillan, Paul Tillman, Beth Martin and Jess Ballenger reviewed drafts of the text, and Barbara Muller served as copyeditor.

I am indebted to Walter Blake, Jaco Cilliers, Mary Hodem and the CRS deputy directors for global solidarity who championed this project, as well as the many overseas staff members who lent their assistance. The following authors, contributors and trouble-shooters have my deep gratitude:

AIDS Office of the Southern African Conference of Catholic Bishops
Christina Auerbach Benavides
Clelia Arguedas
Richard Balmadier
Albert Bisaso
Kathy Brown
Caritas Colombia
Caritas Matagalpa
Joe Carney
John Clossick
CRS Operation Rice Bowl Program
Erica Dahl-Bredine
The Dom Helder Camara Institute
Edwin B. Enping
Daisy Francis
Chris Gilson
Fr. José Alfredo Goncalves

David Heimann
Marina A. Herrera
Human Promotion Of Guaranda
Human Mobility Commission - Honduras
Andar Ismail
Jennifer Jag Jivan
Susan Kadota
Ali Kasum
Nguyen Le Khanh
Yoshut Khemacharo
Chea Muoy Kry
Mexican Episcopal Commission of Youth Ministry - Youth and Migration Program
Youth and Migration Program
Ted Miles
Ligia de Milla
The Missionary Sisters of St. Charles Borromeo (Scalabrinians)
Saah Charles N'Tow
Samalie Odoy
Peace Advocates of Zamboanga
Stela Pijanmanova
Wendell Pierce
Father Ermolao Portella
Cora Tabing-Reyes
José Antonio Cruz Reyes
Carlos G. Rodriguez Rivera, SJ
Martha Ines Romero
Monseñor Pedro Rubiano Sáenz
Carlos Sanchez
Anderi Satya
Michael Sheridan
Ruth Stark
Attique Swati
Tulaha Tahir
Maria Jose Valdivia
Franne VanDerKeilen
Yazmina Zambrano
Andy Zampini, SFO

How To Order

Prayer Without Borders, Celebrating Global Wisdom

. . .makes a unique gift for holidays, birthdays and sacramental celebrations.

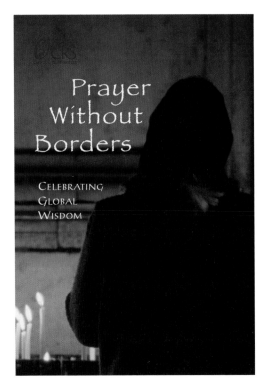

Additional copies can be ordered from SERRV International.

To order by phone call:
800-685-7572

To order on-line visit:
www.SERRV.org

Discounts are available for bulk orders of 20 or more.

To place a bulk order call:
800-685-7572

or for more information email:
orders@serrv.org

For more information on using Prayer Without Borders, Celebrating Global Wisdom visit www.CRSPrayer.org where you'll find:

- Tips and resources for using Prayer Without Borders in your school or faith community.

- Links to CRS programming in the countries represented in the book.

- Information on how CRS helps Catholics in the United States build bridges of solidarity with the people CRS serves overseas.

Notes